At Peace, Filled with Joy

Other Books by Cuong Lu

The Buddha in Jail: Restoring Lives, Finding Hope and Freedom

Happiness Is Overrated: Simple Lessons on Finding Meaning in Each Moment

Wait: A Love Letter to Those in Despair

At Peace, Filled with Joy

BUDDHIST WISDOM FROM THE *DHAMMAPADA*

Cuong Lu

SHAMBHALA

Shambhala Publications, Inc.
2129 13th Street
Boulder, Colorado 80302
www.shambhala.com

Cover art: TropicalPB / Shutterstock
Cover design: Daniel Urban-Brown
Interior design: Gopa & Ted2, Inc.

9 8 7 6 5 4 3 2 1
First Edition

Printed in the United States of America

Shambhala Publications makes every effort to print on acid-free, recycled paper.
Shambhala Publications is distributed worldwide by Penguin Random House, Inc., and its subsidiaries.

Library of Congress Cataloging-in-Publication Data
Names: Lu, Cuong, 1968– author
Title: At peace, filled with joy: Buddhist wisdom from the Dhammapada / Cuong Lu.
Description: Boulder: Shambhala Publications, 2026. | Includes bibliographical references.
Identifiers: LCCN 2025051092 | ISBN 9781645474968 trade paperback
Subjects: LCSH: Religious life—Buddhism. | Peace—Religious aspects—Buddhism. | Theravāda Buddhism—Doctrines.
Classification: LCC BQ7285 .L83 2026
LC record available at https://lccn.loc.gov/2025051092

The authorized representative in the EU for product safety and compliance is eucomply OÜ, Pärnu mnt 139b-14, 11317 Tallinn, Estonia, hello@eucompliancepartner.com.

Contents

Prologue

SOMETIMES our deepest struggles are the very ground from which happiness can grow. Even—perhaps especially—in the midst of suffering, we can find ways to embrace life and attain real peace, clarity, and joy. This book is an invitation to that path of awakening.

The *Dhammapada* is one of the most beautiful, enduring collections of the Buddha's teachings. *Dhamma* in Pali means "the teachings" or "the Way." *Pada* means "footstep" or "path." The word *Dhammapada*, then, can be understood as "The Path of the Dharma." My teacher, Thich Nhat Hanh, wrote, "There is no doubt that the 423 verses of the *Dhammapada* contain the authentic teachings of the Buddha. When we read and contemplate this book, we touch seeds of understanding and love that are buried deep inside of us, and we help them grow."[1]

I studied as a monastic under Thich Nhat Hanh for sixteen years and then practiced what I learned at the monastery as a prison chaplain. In *At Peace, Filled with Joy*, I offer fifty-seven verses from the *Dhammapada*, each followed by a Zen Key and a Reflection based on my experiences as a monk and a chaplain and also as a husband, father, and twenty-first-century citizen. The keys open us to the insights of Zen, pointing toward presence, freedom, and nonduality. The reflections offer ways we can bring the teachings of the *Dhammapada* into daily life, suggesting how we might live with understanding, stability, and compassionate action. Together, the verses, the keys, and the reflections offer a path that can lead from confusion to clarity, from suffering to wisdom, from despair to joy.

Instead of avoiding pain or trying to get rid of suffering, we can learn to stay present with it. When suffering is *held* with understanding, it becomes a teacher. Each chapter is a stepping stone, a way to meet life *as it is* and discover the freedom that is already available. Through this approach, drawn from the ancient words of the Buddha and the living spirit of Zen, we can learn to be at peace, filled with joy, without needing to escape from life or to fix anything.

At Peace, Filled with Joy is divided into four parts, each reflecting a different movement of the heart on its journey home:

Part 1, "Opposites," reminds us how often we are

caught in the struggle between right and wrong, between self and other, between holding on and letting go. All of these opposites are manifestations of a single mind.

Part 2, "The Great Silence," brings us to a place where all ideas dissolve. Language no longer clings to sound but resonates with absolute silence. It is here that we glimpse the most authentic nature of mind.

Part 3, "The Wisdom of Flowers," speaks of a deep connection between human beings and the natural world. It is a place where wisdom is quietly present in you and also in every flower and pebble around you. This wisdom is the mystery that underlies nondiscrimination.

Part 4, "Liberation," describes the moment when we are no longer torn between the shore of ignorance and the shore of awakening. Our boat no longer drifts between suffering and happiness but brings us across the river and back to ourselves.

Please read this book slowly, knowing you are already whole and awake. Listen to each verse as though it's spoken in your own voice. Let each reflection resonate with your unique and precious wisdom. When you read in this way, the book is no longer mine. It's yours. You become the author, the one who remembers what you've always known to be true. Then, even in the midst of chaos and grief, you can return to a place inside that nothing can disturb. In that stillness is peace, and in that clarity is joy.

—Cuong Lu
Magnac-Laval, France
Autumn 2025

Part One

Opposites

Destroying hatred with hatred

Isn't possible.

Only love can transform hate.

This is the eternal law.

—*DHAMMAPADA*, VERSE 5

1
Pure and Impure

Mind is the director,
The master, the creator.
When we speak or act with hatred,
Misery follows, as an ox pulls a cart.

—*DHAMMAPADA*, VERSE 1

Mind is the director,
The master, the creator.
When we speak or act with a pure mind,
Peace is close behind, like a shadow
that follows us everywhere.

—*DHAMMAPADA*, VERSE 2

Zen Key

THE OPENING VERSES of the *Dhammapada* are based on a notion of purity. But Zen teachings remind us that an impure mind is important, too. Hatred is the other side of the coin of peace. If you read these verses dualistically, you will surely choose peace and purity. But hatred and despair have their place. Non-peace can show us the way to peace. Peace and conflict *inter-are*.

After his enlightenment, the Buddha taught that suffering is an ennobling truth. He did not say suffering is a problem to solve or an obstacle to overcome. He didn't say we need to be happy all the time. Recognizing the presence of suffering, he explained, is the first noble truth. We can say hello to misery just as we'd say hello to peace. Seeing the ways a so-called "impure mind" affects us is an important practice. The *Dhammapada* begins with this challenge.

Reflection

We don't need to *try* to be happy. By slowing down and *being ourselves*, we're already contributing to inner peace and peace in the world. Wisdom and happiness are our birthrights. You are already a buddha, and the world needs buddhas now more than ever.

Most of us are trapped in ignorance, fighting within ourselves and with others. To find peace, we only have to be ourselves and let others be themselves. Speaking and acting with a "Big Mind" that includes purity and impurity, you are a buddha, and you recognize others as buddhas, too. This is not a pipe dream. With insight, it can become a shimmering reality.

A student told me, "My suffering comes from others." I said, "No, it comes from your mind." Our minds produce suffering. They are like factories, always working, producing judgments, comparisons, fears, and regrets. They generate the idea "They hurt me. They are the cause." But that idea is painful, and it's manufactured. Still, we believe it. The mind that creates suffering needs to identify a perpetrator. But when we realize that mind is at the root of it all, we stop looking for someone to blame and instead look inward. Only then is healing possible. And the mind not only produces suffering; it produces happiness as well.

When we think happiness is *better than* suffering, we're declaring war within ourselves. When we *know* that happiness and suffering are both truths, peace becomes possible. There's no need to push away impurity. Hold it gently. Even ill will wants to be understood. When you hold the whole coin in your hand—heads and tails—you're no longer divided or afraid. You are beyond pure or impure.

We become pure by embracing impurity, by seeing that even our darkest feelings are not separate from the Dharma. Who we are, right now, with our greed, anger, and confusion, is the raw material of awakening. We don't need to be different from this. The point is awareness.

Your anger, your jealousy, your fear are not enemies to be conquered but doorways to enter, and when we look inside, we'll see understanding and love. If you can stay present with dark emotions long enough, you'll see that they aren't solid. They rise and fall like waves, and what remains is vast and still. This is the stillness of your true nature.

To look at discomfort with clarity is to walk the Buddha's path. To smile at your suffering, not in denial but in recognition, is the first step of liberation. What you think makes you "less than" or "too much" is, in fact, an entry point. What you think is too ugly, too heavy, or too impure is the very place from which wisdom blooms. Impurity is a mirror that reflects back our deepest longings—to come home to ourselves, to be real, and to feel complete. Purity is not the absence of impurity. It is the fullness of being.

2
Blaming and Arguing

He yelled at me. He hit me.
He attacked and robbed me.
Holding hatred in your heart
Can never bring peace.

—*DHAMMAPADA*, VERSE 3

He yelled at me. He hit me.
He attacked and robbed me.
When you release your grudges,
Hatred dissolves by itself.

—*DHAMMAPADA*, VERSE 4

Zen Key

We don't need to remove suffering to be happy. We can look at our suffering as it is and smile. This is called "being with suffering," and with this habit, we don't need to blame others for our suffering or look outside ourselves for happiness. Practicing mindfulness and compassion, we can release the grip our grievances have on us. Holding on to them harms only us, not the other person. When we can let go of our anger and *be peace*, wisdom and compassion arise naturally.

Reflection

All wars begin inside us. They come from misunderstandings based on misperceptions. We navigate the world through images and don't see things as they are. Images are interpretations of past experiences. They're like pictures whose frames don't fit, and we see only a small part of the picture. We hold on to the past to protect us from what seems dangerous, and we think the danger is outside of us. But the feelings that arise are just messengers trying to tell us something. Difficulties aren't obstacles; they're opportunities to understand ourselves better and to understand the root of our pain. And in the process of discovery, we become aware of our strengths and find clarity.

I heard Thich Nhat Hanh say, many times, "Understanding is the other name for love. If you cannot *understand*, you cannot love." Every breath, every step, and every act radiates light. You cannot release grudges on demand, but you can pay attention to what's going on within you and around you, and slowly your grudges may dissolve. The *Dhammapada* teaches that only love can transform hatred.

Grudges and other dark emotions lose their grip on us when we shine the light of attention on them. When we become present with our pain, something inside us shifts. We stop blaming others and start listening to what our heart is reflecting. Sometimes the request is simple: to be seen, feel safe, or be loved. When we listen to this voice within, we become a participant in our own healing and are no longer a victim. We can prolong the cycle of pain or interrupt it with loving attention. We have a choice.

You don't need to be perfect; you just need to be you. Breathe mindfully and notice the places inside you that are constricted, shaking, or numb. Place your attention there. This is a way to take responsibility for the freedom you long for. When you see that you are already whole, you stop organizing your life around the wound.

When Thich Nhat Hanh performed wedding ceremonies, he'd always ask the couple to recite the Five Awarenesses. The fifth is: "Blaming and arguing never help us and only create a wider gap between us; that only understanding, trust, and love can help us change and grow." This is an important practice.

3
Staying Open to Life

Destroying hatred with hatred
Isn't possible.
Only love can transform hate.
This is the eternal law.
—*DHAMMAPADA*, VERSE 5

We forget that
Sooner or later, we'll all pass away.
When we acknowledge this, without flinching,
Conflicts can resolve themselves.
—*DHAMMAPADA*, VERSE 6

Zen Key

THE BUDDHA TAUGHT the "truth of suffering," but we mustn't forget that love is also a truth. These two truths—love and suffering—are partners.

When we suffer, we understand love, and when we understand love, we will choose not to add to anyone's suffering, including our own. Conflicts are resolved first in our own heart. This is key for transformation. And when we know deeply that we'll all pass away sooner or later, we will discover compassion for ourselves and for others.

Reflection

A few years ago, a dear friend suffered a heart attack, and it hurt me, because there is no boundary between us. If we think another person's pain is not our own, we don't understand life. Their happiness is our happiness, and *their suffering is our suffering*. When we realize the extent to which we're connected, we don't need to ask what to do. We just act from our heart, and what happens next is always a surprise. We are bigger than we've ever imagined. I messaged my friend's wife at the hospital that I was there with them.

Every day, we learn from life, not only from things that go well but from the things that go badly, too. My friend's heart attack reminded me how much I cherish him. When you love someone and they're having a hard time, you may discover something about them and about yourself that you had overlooked. The more we care about others, the more we're able to open to life.

When we remember that we'll all pass away, conflicts fall into perspective.

You are an expression of life itself, and after you pass away—no longer manifesting in this form—you and I will still be connected. We're not just here; we're also there and everywhere. You may think I'm in a different place from you on our blue planet, but it's not true. I am *with* you. You, your beloved, and your child are not limited to a particular form or location. We are all wondrous expressions of life; we are everywhere.

Thich Nhat Hanh died in 2022 at the age of ninety-five. My father passed away earlier. But, to me, they are still here, in my voice, the way I hold my body, and in each breath. When I look at trees, I see them. When I bow, they bow with me. When you touch the esence of life, you touch all those who have gone before and all those yet to come. Nothing is ever lost.

Knowing that we will pass away is not meant to make us afraid. It's a way to encourage us to love more deeply, to stop delaying peace, to look at our loved ones and say what we need to say. We don't have to agree with everything everyone does. We can love them as they are, and this verse reminds us to do so before it's too late. When you hold their hand, hold it fully. When you listen, listen with your whole body. We don't know how long we have. Life is fragile. Fragility is what allows us to see the preciousness of everything.

Sometimes we try to protect ourselves from pain by shutting down. But dissociating doesn't protect us; it isolates us further. It may have been an important survival strategy at some point in our lives, but usually it's a reminder that we need to observe what in this moment feels threatening and whether it's true. Usually it's a reflex, not a response to danger in the present. Knowing how to navigate these states of our nervous system, we can begin, slowly, to stay open to life as it is and to let both joy and sorrow move us. It means knowing that suffering and happiness are both a part of life. When grief arrives, let it arrive. When love arrives, let it arrive. That is easier said than done. Mindful breathing and a moment of pause can help. The more porous you are, the more alive you will feel. And over time, you will feel safe to open, and it will help others feel safe when they're with you.

4
Real Happiness

Those who indulge—
Overeating or drinking too much,
Those who are lazy or immoderate,
Will be vanquished by Mara the tempter,
As the wind snaps off the weak limbs of a tree.

—*DHAMMAPADA*, VERSE 7

Those who live mindfully—
Seeing clearly, eating and drinking in moderation,
Living with faith, practicing diligently,
Cannot be touched by Mara.
These Way-Seekers are like mountains,
Unshakable, even in the wildest of storms.

—*DHAMMAPADA*, VERSE 8

Zen Key

THE DALAI LAMA wrote, "A tree with strong roots can withstand the most violent storm, but the tree can't grow roots [if it waits until] the storm appears on the horizon."[2] Michael Kearney, who teaches "luminous resilience," comments, "We are already in the midst of violent storms of war, wealth inequality, discrimination, and an escalating climate crisis. We need to begin growing roots now, so when the winds get even stronger, we're stronger too."[3]

The United States Declaration of Independence speaks of an "inalienable right" to happiness. But sometimes we try to satisfy ourselves *at the expense of others*. To experience real happiness, we need to care for ourselves while being mindful of others and not exploiting the environment. When we live in this way, our mind will be steady and those we care about will be well, too. We need to be solid as a mountain and steady as the rain so we can embrace life to its fullest.

Reflection

We have the ability to feel alive, receive what life offers, and savor each moment. But sometimes we draw too impenetrable a line between our life and the lives of others. We think, "This is mine," not considering the well-being of others and even separating ourselves from Mother Earth, and we wreak havoc.

During the Vietnam War, Americans dropped Agent

Orange throughout the country of my birth, knowing that its active ingredient, dioxin, causes cancer, neurological disorders, and birth defects in those not yet born. The consequences of their actions are still visible. How can anyone do things they know will cause so much harm? The answer is in the *Dhammapada*. We cause damage when we're self-serving at the expense of others, and it turns out, it's also at the expense of ourselves. "Those who are lazy or immoderate will be vanquished by Mara the tempter." Without discipline, our insight and compassion remain undeveloped, and we focus solely on what we crave for our own body and mind, as if we're separate from the rest of creation.

When we act selfishly, we struggle. We hold on to our fear and anger, and they weigh us down. Conversely, the more we support others, the lighter we feel. When our energy isn't flowing, we're prone to illness. When we know what's true and stop swimming against the current, we're able to contribute to others and have fewer blockages within. Love is the most intelligent investment. The more we care about others, the healthier we'll be. If we're unhappy, it means we're comparing our *idea* of happiness to what's in front of us. Real happiness is never based on an image. Real happiness has no cause; *it just is*.

When we chase pleasure at the expense of others'

needs, something essential is lost. True happiness arises when we care for ourselves *and* our environment. Living this way, we feel whole, relaxed, and focused. Relationships deepen, and the world we cherish will begin to recover. In the monastery, when we walked slowly and ate our meals in silence, we could witness life unfolding on its own. At times, one morsel of food reveals how complete this moment is, that nothing is missing. Joy isn't just up the road. It lives in each breath, each step, each awake gaze. But if we try to hold on to them, they'll fade. The beauty is in enjoying them and then letting them pass. Joy doesn't demand perfection. It asks only that we see and feel.

Moderation isn't just restraint; it's also freedom. When we live with care and discipline, we can touch the fullness of life, and generosity flows like a river. We stop "consuming" and begin nourishing and being nurtured. This happiness cannot be taken from us. It's already present. When we know that we are already enough, we don't have to chase happiness; we only need to arrive.

5
The Art of Doing Nothing

The one who wears monastic robes,
While his mind is mired in confusion,
Not modulating his impulses
Is unworthy of being called a monk.

—*DHAMMAPADA*, VERSE 9

Whoever leaves dishonesty behind
And practices sincerely,
Not manipulating and living in truth
Is worthy of Buddha's robe.

—*DHAMMAPADA*, VERSE 10

Zen Key

THESE VERSES ARE about courage—the courage to stay present even with confusion. Honesty and sincerity do not require the absence of confusion. We all feel overwhelmed at times. The practice is to see your confusion, not to suppress it. Confusion will recede by itself when you're brave enough to see things as they are, even when they are different from your preconceptions.

In former times, only those who lived a monastic life were considered true practitioners. Today, if you practice sincerely, you too are a student of the Way. Even confusion can lead to peace. We can't live twenty-four hours a day without any confusion at all. We make mistakes, and we can learn from them. The practice is to say hello to greed, hatred, and confusion every time we notice their presence. And we can say hello to clarity and conviction when they're there, too. We observe how we feel when we are practicing earnestly and how we feel when we aren't.

Reflection

Our mind likes to judge things as good or bad. Compassion, loving-kindness, and forgiveness are "good," and anger, jealousy, and hatred are "bad." If increasing the good and decreasing the bad is your practice, you'll spend a lot of time wearing the robes of a judge. This is the opposite of nondiscrimination, which is an important teaching of the Buddha. Life isn't always "good." We don't need to be what others want us to be, or vice versa. Looking at what's "bad" with insight can be fruitful when we look hard enough.

When someone tells me they're never angry, I don't feel reassured. When they're angry at me, I say, "Thank you," because their anger tells me about them and about me. Anger is an opportunity to understand and appreciate each other. We want to understand our beloved's anger, so we listen to them and learn what they're going through. There's room in our heart for them without needing to lessen their anger or rescue them. That is the art of doing nothing, which comes from understanding. If we can tolerate their anger, before we know it a smile will appear on their face. The trick is to see beneath the anger.

I worked as a spiritual counselor at a men's prison and had one-on-one meetings with murderers and rapists. But I didn't see them as murderers or rapists. I saw buddhas, and I suggested we sit together in silence. As we did so, I felt their pain and suffering, and at the same time I saw buddhas who had a lot of insight and peace. I saw the dark and the light, and I had complete confidence in each of them. Most of these men needed only twenty minutes to discover their own peace and stability.

If you cannot see another person's wisdom and stability, they might see themselves as "bad" for a lifetime and suffer from guilt, self-loathing, and regret. But if you see a buddha in the other person, if you see that they're beautiful just as they are, they can begin to feel safe and whole in just twenty minutes. When we look closely at anyone without being caught by images, we always end up feeling admiration.

Look in the mirror and while you do, let go of all your ideas about yourself. Say farewell to your self-image and just see yourself as you are, without trying to change a thing. The spiritual path is to discover who you are. Now look at others as though you're looking at a buddha. They can feel it.

As long as we think we're a self without knowing we're also a non-self, we'll continue to hurt others. The way to peace is to discover generosity, or *dana paramita*. When you no longer feel like a victim or a perpetrator, you'll discover generosity. You can be open and kind with others because you know that you're a beautiful buddha who has a lot to give. Your being already contains all the causes and conditions of enlightenment. There is nothing to fix. There is only something to see.

Sometimes to help someone, you only need to be with them in silence. Stay present with them in their confusion. You don't need to turn away or bring light into the room. Light appears just from your staying. An empty cup is useful because it holds space. You, too, can hold space. You don't need a robe to do that.

When you stop needing others to be different, they change. When you stop needing yourself to be better, you grow. This is the paradox of the spiritual path: We arrive by stopping, not by striving. Doing nothing requires *trust* that the Buddha is still alive in you and the willingness to be present, even for a few minutes. Doing this can change your life.

6
Are You Sure?

Those who think what's not true to be true,
Or what's not real to be real,
Can't touch what's essential.
They simply lack discernment.

—*DHAMMAPADA*, VERSE 11

When something's true and they know it's true,
When it's not true and they know it's not true,
Through clear thinking and honest conduct,
They can attain peace.

—*DHAMMAPADA*, VERSE 12

Zen Key

EVERYTHING CHANGES. The Buddha identified change, not-self, and suffering as the Dharma Seals, or marks of existence. As we know from physics, all is in flux. Knowing this, why do we think we can grasp truth as something solid and unwavering? What if the things we hold on to as true are not true? The Buddha encourages us to look at everything anew. As Thich Nhat Hanh often said, "Are you sure?"

Thich Nhat Hanh wrote about this in *The Diamond That Cuts Through Illusion*:

> When you look at your close friend, you may think you understand her completely, but that is difficult because *she is a river of reality*. In every moment, dharmas that are not her enter and leave her. You cannot take hold of her. By observing her form, feelings, perceptions, mental formations, and consciousness, you can see that she is here sitting next to you, *and she is elsewhere at the same time*. She is in the present, the past, and the future. Your friend . . . cannot be grasped because [she has] no beginning and no end. [Her] presence is deeply connected to all dharmas, all objects of mind in the universe.[4]

Reflection

To attain clarity and insight, we need to widen our path so we can touch multiple truths at the same time. All that we experience in life—what we see, hear, taste, smell, and touch—are created by consciousness. When we're caught by illusory thinking, thinking what is unreal to be real, we are fooling ourselves. With training and honesty, we can discern the truth *and* act authentically.

Jesus said, "I am the way, the truth, and the life."[5] He was preaching to those who believed in an almighty God, and so when he added this revolutionary statement—"When you look at me, you see God, and when you look at yourself, you see me"[6]—he brought them closer to God. Today, however, when people are less certain about the form of God, we might change Jesus's statement to, "*You* are the way, the truth, and the life."

All too often, we imagine truth as something we have to seek, something distant or grand. But what if truth is already present, simple and near? The sound of a teacup on the table, the sigh of the person sitting next to you, the ache in your back. These are not obstacles to truth; they are expressions of it. Truth is not hidden in scriptures or carved in stone. It is alive in each of us. It moves in our breath, in our silence, and in the ways we care. When we look with clarity, we don't just see the world, we see the one observing the world, too. This is the beginning of insight.

I sometimes feel more truth in a moment of care than in a thousand beliefs. A man once wept in my arms, not because of something I'd said but because I didn't turn away. Truth seeks intimacy. You don't need to hold the same views as another person to be joined in the heart. In fact, the more we let go of views, the more space there is for understanding. And in that opening, life can enter. To live in truth is to be fully yourself—not performing, just being. Only then will you see that you're not separate from the earth, your ancestors, or each other. The light that moved through Jesus also moves through you.

When we live with disregard for others and the earth, we all suffer. But if we are truly present with all that surrounds us, our inner turmoil ceases. We can be present for our pain and the pain of others, as well. Truth is found in connection. When I connect with you, I connect with the Buddha and I connect with God. Allowing another person in, we invite all of life in, and we're no longer alone or lonely. Your happiness is my happiness. Together, we can build a sustainable world. If you are the Way, let each step manifest it. If you are the truth, let each breath express it. If you are the life, take good care of all beings.

7
Living in the Past

Like a poorly thatched house
Which rain pours through,
The untrained mind
Is flooded with obsession.

—*DHAMMAPADA*, VERSE 13

Like a well-thatched house,
That rain can't penetrate,
The well-cultivated mind
Is free from compulsion.

—*DHAMMAPADA*, VERSE 14

Zen Key

ACCORDING TO Buddhist psychology, emotions are expressions of consciousness. These emotions are stored in our root consciousness and affect how we perceive ourselves and others. With practice, we can learn to recognize that all emotions are neutral and equal. This is essential for reducing suffering and promoting peace. In the *Dhammapada,* the Buddha calls this "training the mind."

Reflection

When we study Abhidharma, Buddhist psychology, we explore the relationship between consciousness (*vijñana*) and the self (*atman*). Where there is perception, there is always an idea of the self that prevents us from seeing the true nature of reality, what Suzuki Roshi called "things as it is." Looking through the filter of the self, we think we're seeing others, but we see only ourselves.

Images are always based in the past. Because we see through the lens of our storehouse of images, it's difficult to see with fresh eyes. We see the present as an update of the past, not as something fresh and new. To avoid being run by negative states, we try to be positive. But positive causes are no different from negative ones. They're all images. When people call us smart or beautiful, we believe them because we want to see ourselves as smart or beautiful. But it's a choice. When advertisers flatter us, we feel affirmed. But their sales pitch will have no effect on us if we understand the role of images in perception. When we know our mind, it's like having a well-thatched roof that the rain cannot penetrate.

We can begin by noticing how often we're not actually present. We just reconjure the past. A word someone says triggers an old wound, and we feel judged. When we meet someone, we see our early version of them based on memory, fear, desire, and habit. So we respond to a story we've created and think it's truth. When you notice that happening, take a mindful breath and recognize that you're looking through a filter. When you do, the focus will begin to soften. We don't need to discard the past. The past arises to help us be safe. But we need to stop thinking that the contents of our store consciousness are the whole picture. Something new is also happening and worthy of our attention. We can, in conversation with the past, determine how to proceed. And we can do this while staying deeply present with ourselves and others.

When we encounter someone with no agenda, something within us opens. We hear not just their words but their silence too. We feel their presence, and true awareness arises. In that moment, praise and blame lose their power. We're not swayed by promises or manipulated by fear. We feel steady, not through an image of strength, but because we're free of the need to posture. When we're not living in the past, we can truly see—and be seen.

8
Manas Creates Everything

Sad today and sad tomorrow,
The dishonest are doubly forlorn:
Sad about their mind-state
And regretful of their actions.

—*DHAMMAPADA*, VERSE 15

Happy now and happy in the future,
The honest are happy twice:
At peace, filled with joy
Pleased with their lives

—*DHAMMAPADA*, VERSE 16

Zen Key

SADNESS AND HAPPINESS come from the same place in our mind. Buddhist psychology speaks of *alayavijñana*, storehouse, or store, consciousness. And the "I" that fetches memories or ideas from store consciousness is called *manas*. We can't live a life just of sadness or just of happiness. Both poles of the dyad are always present. If we want only happiness, when suffering comes, we suffer twice, "doubly forlorn" as verse 15 points out. When we accept both joy and sorrow as parts of life, the *Dhammapada* calls this being happy twice—now and in the future.

Reflection

Dharma with a capital *D* is the teaching of the Buddha, and dharma with a small *d* means a manifestation or a phenomenon. In Abhidharma, one of the eight consciousnesses is called manas. It is like the ego in Western psychology. It helps establish boundaries to keep us safe, but at the same time, it views the world through the lens of personal history, making it difficult to see things freshly. Manas gives us the feeling that we're separate, and it judges things to determine whether they're safe or unsafe, helpful or harmful. Manas is like the head of the family protecting us, while at the same time not giving us space to express anything outside the known "truths" of the family system.

We are so accustomed to the voice of manas, it can be difficult to recognize it, and so we follow it blindly. If we feel angry about something someone did to us years ago, manas waters a seed in our alayavijñana, and anger arises. We feel the past as a fact, and we suffer even though it's all taking place inside of us.

But we have agency, and with meditation and perseverance, we can witness the process—the way the past colors our perceptions and how reflexively it shapes our actions. We don't have to navigate the world using dated maps. These two verses of the *Dhammapada* tell us that we *can* see things as they are and make life choices based on current data rather than old photo albums. Until we become conscious that these dated images are guiding our responses, we will keep doing the same things over and over, regardless of the consequences. Still, manas is not our enemy. It simply wants us to be safe. But its boundaries become prisons when we can't see beyond them. We don't need to fight manas, but we do need to see it. Recognizing a seed before it blossoms into reactivity, we're already free.

Sometimes pausing is enough. Manas whispers, *You cannot trust him*, or *Defend yourself from her*, or *You're not enough*, and instead of allowing these statements to be taken as gospel, we can return to our breath and ask, *Am I sure? Is it true?* Asking questions like these opens a door, and through that door, life enters. We don't need to destroy old seeds. But we do need to discern which seeds to water. What we water, grows. If we water the seeds of presence, courage, and compassion, these seeds will support us when the old films play again. We don't need to destroy the films; we only need to see the projector.

We can acknowledge how these films and photo albums are trying to protect us and let them know they have served their purpose, and now we're choosing something new. We don't need to forget the past, but we do want to make decisions based on the present. Doing this, we are happy twice, entering the present moment fully and allowing new ways of being in the world.

9
Actions Have Consequences

Those who act with ill-intent
Experience suffering now and in the future.
They cannot forget the evil acts they've committed
Now or forever.

—*DHAMMAPADA*, VERSE 17

Those who act kindly
Reap happiness now and in the future.
They always remember their actions,
And feel joy wherever they go.

—*DHAMMAPADA*, VERSE 18

Zen Key

THERE IS A teaching in early Buddhism called the five remembrances. The fifth of these is, "My actions are my only true belongings. I cannot escape the consequences of my actions. My actions are the ground on which I stand."[7]

According to this teaching, our fate is not determined by things outside of us. Actions initiated by will or volition (*chetana*) have consequences, which are called karma fruit (*karmaphala*). This verse describes how beneficial actions yield beneficial fruit and harmful actions generate problems.

Reflection

Although we are influenced by past actions and by our lineage, epigenetics, and social environment, we can still choose love. We always have options, even after committing unwholesome acts. We can learn from our mistakes and even come to see those who have harmed us as buddhas. We can forgive others and even ourselves. Transformation is possible.

Forgiveness is not *erasing* pain or pretending what happened never happened. Forgiveness is seeing the past clearly and choosing to release the links in the karmic chain that bind us. When we forgive, we are not condoning, we are choosing to be free of it. Just saying "I want to want to forgive" can be an opening. But we need to forgive ourselves first.

When I sat with prisoners—men who had committed real harm and who society had cast out—I sat with their pain, and in doing so, I saw the possibility of their wholeness. As mentioned, sometimes just twenty minutes of real presence—being seen without judgment—was enough for release to take place.

We can always act with love. We can always choose not to harm. In every moment, we get to water seeds of goodness again. And when we don't feel ready to choose love, we can sit with the intention and whisper to ourselves, "I am not bound by yesterday." Doing this is revolutionary. The Buddha taught us not to be prisoners of the past. Each moment is a gate, and what awaits us on the other side is not perfection but peace.

10
Seeing with Insight

Being erudite about the teachings
Without actually practicing them
Is like counting your neighbor's cows
Without tasting their milk.

—*DHAMMAPADA*, VERSE 19

Those who don't talk about the teachings
But practice them,
Releasing greed, hatred, and ignorance
Attain liberation of mind
And enjoy the bountiful harvest of
a life well-lived.

—*DHAMMAPADA*, VERSE 20

Zen Key

ONE DAY, St. Francis of Assisi saw an almond tree in the middle of winter, and he said, "Brother Almond Tree, talk to me of God." Suddenly flowers burst forth from the branches, and the tree was filled with fragrant blossoms.[8] If you look at a deciduous tree in winter, you won't see any leaves or flowers. But the tree isn't dead. Its wisdom is knowing when to be dormant and when to spring forth. If you look beneath the level of expression, you may see the almond tree's leaves and flowers bursting forth year-round, even in the midst of winter.

Reflection

We have the ability to recognize truth even when it's not apparent. That is "seeing with insight." Those with insight are grateful much of the time, even when others are not doing what we want them to. With insight, we have a clear connection to our roots.

It's like always being tuned in or surfing the web. Some say the "wood wide web" is a vast, interconnected network of fungi in the soil, composed primarily of mycelium, that links trees and plants together. This network allows for the exchange of nutrients, water, and even chemical signals, facilitating communication and resource sharing among organisms in an ecosystem. When we tune in to the wood wide web, we can see more deeply. The password, I believe, is URMe. Practicing the Way of the Buddha (and the mycelia), we see with insight and enjoy the fruit (and leaves and flowers) of a life well-lived.

Insight doesn't require ideal conditions. It doesn't need silence or a retreat. Sometimes it appears in the midst of chaos, when you're angry, tired, or afraid. It whispers, *This, too, is part of the path.* When we see with insight, we stop asking, *Why is this happening to me?* and begin asking, *What is this offering me?* Questioning opens the heart, softens the grip of self-centeredness, and connects us back to the web of life. When we see with insight, we don't look for reasons to be grateful; we simply recognize that everything belongs. When we feel resistance, we know that life is challenging us. We don't need to agree with every download. We just need to meet them all with attention.

There's a difference between knowing the Dharma and living it. Talking about compassion is easy, but staying open while someone is criticizing us takes practice. To teach mindfulness is not the same as breathing through disappointment without shutting down. Insight makes moments like these possible. Nothing needs to be pushed away.

And sometimes, when you see with insight, you laugh spontaneously. Not because life is funny, but because you feel free. Even when things fall apart, even when you're not sure if the ground beneath you is still there, you can still laugh. It's the quiet joy that comes with insight. We don't practice to escape or show off. We practice to arrive fully into our own life.

Part Two

The Great Silence

Those who meditate regularly
Persevering with diligence
Enjoy Nirvana, the Silence,
And experience supreme peace

—*DHAMMAPADA*, VERSE 23

11
A Daily Practice

Those who meditate regularly
Persevering with diligence
Enjoy Nirvana, the Silence,
And experience supreme peace.

—*DHAMMAPADA*, VERSE 23

They make an effort to stay mindful,
Pure and prudent in their actions.
Living mindfully in accord with the Dharma,
Their loving-kindness grows each day.

—*DHAMMAPADA*, VERSE 24

Zen Key

MINDFULNESS, supported by insight, is at the center of Zen practice. Mindfulness brings us closer to ourselves and helps us not dwell in distraction. With mindfulness, concentration, and insight, we can enjoy each moment of life.

Meditation can be highly beneficial. You sit upright in a chair or on a cushion, aware of each in-breath and out-breath. And you can continue to practice mindful awareness all day long. It's not difficult to touch Nirvana, the Great Silence, this way, but sustaining it can be a challenge.

During the war in Vietnam, Thich Nhat Hanh helped start a movement that became known as "engaged Buddhism." It was a continuation of the practices of the Buddha, meant for challenging times. We apply the insights we gain from mindfulness to everything we do and become a resource to those who are suffering. In his book *Peace Is Every Step*, Thich Nhat Hanh wrote, "Mindfulness must be engaged."

Reflection

Engaged Buddhism is practiced in everyday life. Thich Nhat Hanh—who we call Thây, meaning "teacher"—taught us mindful breathing with a smile to help us touch happiness. As his student, his "continuation," I want to add—or actually, subtract—something. I believe that you don't have to *do* anything at all. Rather than practicing what Thây called "mouth yoga" to touch happiness, you can discover that you are already happy. You may think practice means effort, but what if practice means stopping because you've already arrived? You don't need to breathe mindfully to be happy. You can breathe mindfully *because* you're happy.

Doing nothing, not out of laziness but out of trust that your breath knows the way, is radical. You don't need to force insight. It will come like a seed sprouting in fertile soil. You don't even need to chant, sit, or even "practice." When you open a window and feel the breeze touch your skin, put your hand on your heart and truly feel your own presence. That's all.

Tears can be more honest than a smile. Sometimes crying is the deepest practice. It means you have arrived, and your heart is open again.

12
Agitation

The mind quakes
So much that it's hard to rein in.
The wise ones learn to focus
Their minds to be straight as an arrow.

—*DHAMMAPADA*, VERSE 33

Like a fish out of water
Thrown onto shore,
This mind quivers
Under the power of Mara.

—*DHAMMAPADA*, VERSE 34

Zen Key

WHEN YOU FEEL disturbed and nothing seems to calm you, return to your breathing. Conscious breathing can "straighten" your mind and bring it back into focus. When you practice this way, you can withstand the power of Mara, the devilish being who tried to stop

Siddhartha Gautama from attaining enlightenment. The monk Nyanaponika describes Mara as "the personification of the forces antagonistic to enlightenment."[9]

Only insight can destroy Mara's power. Come back to yourself, breathe mindfully, and know that you are strong enough to stay present, even in the midst of suffering and confusion.

Reflection

Hatred, anxiety, and agitation can last a lifetime and can feel as if they'll never disappear. Perhaps we were screamed at, abused, or betrayed, and the damage feels baked in. Still, the Buddha teaches that transformation is possible. As Dr. Gabor Maté says, "Trauma is not what happens to you, it's what happens inside you."[10] With awareness, we can begin to change our response.

We usually think events that have already taken place are unchangeable. But if quantum physics is correct and time is not sequential, and if the Buddha's teaching that everything is subject to change is true, it is possible for conditioned causes to transform and for overwhelming feelings to ease. When we're triggered, these emotions may flare up and make us feel powerless again. Until we see the true nature of what happened—and continues to happen—inside us, we'll remain the victim of events.

Don't misunderstand the *Dhammapada*'s teaching that hatred can only be overcome by love or Jesus's teaching to turn the other cheek. Love is truly love only when it's accompanied by awareness.

When you light a match, the flame will burn for as long as there is fuel. Both oxygen and a flammable material are necessary for a fire to burn. When conditions are no longer sufficient to keep the flame alive, it will be extinguished. The fires of rage will continue to burn only if we add fuel to the fire. The moment we discover that hatred is provisional, not permanent, we can be at peace, even if confusion is still present. We think suffering will always be there, but hatred, anger, jealousy, and all states of mind are empty at their core, independent of a separate "self." We don't have to be afraid anymore.

Suffering is inevitable, but it does not have to hurt so much. If, consciously or unconsciously, we are avoiding suffering, we may even believe it isn't there. If we're busy blaming others for our suffering, we probably won't see it. The fuel that powers our suffering is "in the perpetrator's hands," and we suffer because we think our suffering is due to what they did.

But trauma and perpetrator are stored images, and holding tightly to these images, we suffer. Transformation doesn't ask us to erase what happened. It invites us to look again. If we learn to treat conditioned causes as part of the equation and not the whole picture, that in itself will clear the clouds and allow the sun to warm us again. The sun is always there, but it was covered by our notions, making it seem like winter all year round. Without denying what happened in the past or what's happening inside us now, we can look again at our beliefs and try to see things as they are. Doing so, we stop identifying just with the one who was hurt. That self, too, is changing moment by moment.

Some suffering asks to be released and some asks to be held, like a child who needs to cry, rage, or rest. Our inner wounds don't need quick answers. They need someone to stay with them. Awareness is not about fixing. It is about staying long enough for something deeper to be revealed. If we hold too tightly or release too quickly, we may become frozen in time.

Sometimes our shaking, our anxiety, is a release, allowing energies that have been held for years to express themselves. Peter Levine teaches that animals in the wild shake uncontrollably after trauma to release the woundedness. The focus on *overcoming* anxiety, anger, or even being shut down might be misplaced. *Being with* and *allowing* them may be what is needed.

Although we may not be ready to forgive, we can, perhaps, stop telling ourselves the story from a singular point of view. What hurts may not disappear right away, but it might loosen its grip. When we stop interpreting it, we may notice a quiet space within us opening. Sometimes change takes place beneath the radar. After a while, we can feel it in our breathing, in our shoulders, and in the silence that envelops us after years of cacophony.

13
What We Like (and What We Don't)

The mind is difficult to hold.
It's impulsive, a whirlwind of desires.
It can be beneficial to tame the mind.
When the mind is calm, peace is present.

—*DHAMMAPADA*, VERSE 35

The mind is difficult to see.
It's subtle, a whirlwind of desires.
The wise ones protect their minds.
When you protect your mind, peace will follow.

—*DHAMMAPADA*, VERSE 36

Zen Key

OUR MIND IS a vortex of swirling desires. Inner peace is elusive. Chinese ancestor Sengcan said, "The Great Way is not difficult / for those who have no preferences.

/ When love and hate are both absent / everything becomes clear and undisguised. / Make the smallest distinction, however, / and heaven and earth are set infinitely apart."[11]

The practice is to let go of discrimination and guard against ideas that arise from duality—good and bad, right and wrong, like and dislike. When we live with nondiscrimination, peace will come.

Reflection

The Buddha said that suffering has three causes: I want this, I don't want that, and I want more of this and less of that. We consider health, love, and stability to be positive and illness, hatred, and instability to be negative. We think our problem is having too few positives or too many negatives. And we think watering the positive seeds within us will weaken the negative seeds. These, I believe, are mistaken notions. When we strengthen the positive seeds in our store consciousness, we also strengthen the negative seeds. Love causes as much suffering as anger.

When water is stagnant, it starts to smell. When water is flowing, it purifies itself. Emotions are positive when they flow. When emotions are stagnant, they cause pain. It's not about positive or negative; it's about movement, aliveness, and flow. We need love *and* anger, stability *and* stress. What's important is that there is a pathway for our emotions to flow.

When we're stuck, everything hurts. All that comes from stagnancy—positive and negative—makes us ill. The more we grasp happiness and fear suffering, we impede life's flow, and we suffer. Once we become free from discrimination and see happiness even in our suffering, we realize Sengcan's nondiscrimination.

In Zen, we call this "doing nothing, or non-doing." But even when you practice non-doing, you might be trying to amplify the positive and suppress the negative. But we're not just bad or good; we're both. We're beautiful just as we are. If we do nothing for just one minute, we come back to ourselves, our true home. This isn't perfection; it's letting life flow. We don't need to be joyful all the time. We just need to feel, without judgment, whatever is here.

Peace can be a trap, compassion a performance, and joy a mask. They're not wrong, but when we cling to them, they become stagnant. A flower can't always bloom. It needs time to rest, to wilt, and to go underground. Boredom, restlessness, and pain are not mistakes. They're movement. "Doing nothing" disrupts holding on. We are already enough.

A true practitioner of the Way doesn't shine all the

time. Sometimes they stop presenting as a polished self and become like clear water—responsive, unstoppable, and invisible. Don't be afraid of negative emotions. Anger is not the absence of love; it's a cry from a part of us that cares. Sadness is not weakness; it's a manifestation of heartfelt meaning. Let them have their voices. We don't have to fulfill others' expectations to be worthy of taking time off. Resting is our birthright, our original state. When we stop interfering, the Dharma takes care of itself. If we stop focusing on feeling better, we'll be able to breathe again.

14
Tell Your Fear Not to Be Afraid

Far from home, living alone,
Disembodied, or hidden in a cave,
Those who calm the mind
Can break free of Mara's bondage.

—*DHAMMAPADA*, VERSE 37

Those whose minds are agitated
And don't know the Buddha's Way,
Whose composure is shaky,
Their wisdom is still incomplete.

—*DHAMMAPADA*, VERSE 38

Zen Key

SHAKYAMUNI BUDDHA was a human being who attained enlightenment. He is not a god, and because of this, we know that we, too, can become enlightened. We may go on retreats and apply the practices of stillness to tame the mind. When our mind comes to silence, we find that we're in harmony with ourselves and all of nature. We are no longer running after happiness, no longer afraid of life's challenges. Practicing with others or alone at home, we discover our true wisdom.

Reflection

While training as a monk at Plum Village, I learned to let go of thoughts and opinions. It's not that my thoughts and emotions vanished. "Being still and knowing" means staying present with whatever is there, including fear, anxiety, anger, or hatred, not to mention love, happiness, and peace. I learned to observe whatever arose in my mind and body, befriend it, and watch it change.

Insight means to see what is there. When you see fear, you can say, "This is fear," knowing that fear has been created by conditions, some of which are no longer present. All dharmas are empty, like a teacup that has no tea in it. The nature of the cup, its inherent trait, is emptiness. You don't have to do anything with your fear; it too is empty. At times, it seems our fear is permanent, that it will always be here. But if you tell your fear not to be afraid, that it can stay as long as it wants, and then become curious about it, fear will lose its power over you. When you're protected by insight, fear can no longer harm you.

After the Buddha's enlightenment, Mara, the god of death, challenged him: "You think you're so enlightened, Big Shot, but you're not." Buddha replied, simply, "I see you, Mara." With that, Mara left. Don't be afraid. *See* your suffering, fear, hatred, and unrest as companions on the path of awakening. When they are done with you, they will leave, perhaps with a fond farewell, or perhaps they'll just steal away into the night.

You don't have to heal fear. You just have to stop arguing with it. Once fear is seen, it softens. Once it's allowed, it begins to shift. That is the power of stillness. It makes room for transformation not by force but by insight.

Stillness doesn't mean being frozen. It means not being pulled away from what is and remaining open, even when it's uncomfortable. When fear visits, offer it a chair or a cushion and let it sit beside you. Ask what it's trying to protect, and listen to it. Often, fear only wants to be heard.

Awareness is not the end of suffering but the end of being ruled by it. You don't need to disappear Mara to be free. You need to recognize him. When you can say, "I see you," to your own fear, your own rage, your own self-doubt, you take away their disguises. Mara will come again and again, but you know him now. You can greet him instead of panicking. You can breathe instead of arguing. You'll walk with him until he disappears into the next gust of wind.

Insight is not cold or distant. It's warm and steady. It stays with you like a friend. It doesn't rush to fix your sadness or solve your anxiety. It keeps you company until your heart remembers that it's safe. To be still and know is not a passive act. It's the deepest form of courage. You stop hiding. You stop pretending and simply say, "This is what's here." And somehow, that's enough. Stillness is not an escape. Being still is trusting.

15
Timelessness

Those who have awakened,
Whose minds are not filled with desire,
Whose hearts are unburdened,
Unshaken by good or evil,
Are unafraid.

—*DHAMMAPADA*, VERSE 39

The body is fragile, like porcelain.
Knowing this, keep your mind like a fortress.
Fighting Mara with the sword of nondiscrimination,
Protect what you have, without clinging.

—*DHAMMAPADA*, VERSE 40

Zen Key

When we are not caught in duality—good and bad, right and wrong—we touch timelessness (*akalika*). With Manjushri's sword of discerning wisdom, we win all battles—not by choosing sides but, free from greed, hatred, and delusion, by being present with all. At peace with ourselves, there are no enemies.

Reflection

We live with a conventional idea of time. What we've done in the past seems irreversible, and our attachment to the past colors our experience of the present. In fact, there is no separation between past, present, and future; they are deeply connected. Knowing that the past has not really disappeared can help us heal many of our wounds. When we touch the past with insight, it becomes alive again, and what was a burden becomes a source of new understanding. We can, for example, transform guilt into compassion and regret into insight.

My father passed away when I was young. I didn't understand what had happened, so I called out, "Daddy, where are you?" We live in the dimension of manifestation, but there are other dimensions. In the dimension of timelessness, or akalika, there is no past, present, or future and no fear. When you feel unlovable or misunderstood, when you have the feeling you are without a connection to life, you can go to the dimension of timelessness, the dimension of love. It was there that I found my father.

Not long ago I saw my son lighting incense in front

of an altar I'd made for my father. He was communicating with his grandfather, who he'd never met, and it was clear they were in touch. Love is always available. When we feel mired in loneliness, we can turn to the dimension of love and call upon our ancestors. If we listen carefully, we may hear them: "We support you. We want you to be happy again."

Breathing mindfully is an expression of timelessness. We can *feel* the joy of connection. In that dimension, there is no separation between the Buddha and us. It's a practice of loving ourselves. Because of akalika, I can connect with my father and with my teacher, who passed away while I was writing this book.

Peace is not something we create; it's something we remember. Peace is always there, beneath the layers of distraction, beneath the beliefs we've inherited about not being enough. When we rest in timelessness, we see that we are never truly apart from those we love or from the truth of each moment. There are millions of ways to escape suffering. But we don't need to escape. We are already whole and connected with all of life. When we know in our bones that we are naturally peaceful, fear and anger cannot harm us.

To practice akalika is to listen with your whole body. You don't need a mystical experience; you only need to be quiet enough to hear what is always beside you, whispering. When you place a bowl of fruit on the altar as an offering, when you light a stick of incense, when you breathe with the trees, you're not performing an empty ritual. You're opening a door.

Those you miss are not gone. They are living in your actual hands, your speech, and your silence. When you smile, they smile through you. When you take a mindful step, their feet are walking beside yours. There's no need to prove the dimension of timelessness exists. You only need to trust your longing. That is the thread that leads you home. And when you arrive, you realize that you were never alone.

The past can be healed, and the future is being shaped by your presence now. And this moment, if you rest in it deeply, contains all of time. We don't need to escape from or fix anything. We only need to remember who we are and where we've always belonged. This remembering is the heart of waking up.

16
Pause

Sooner or later, this body
Will lie in the ground,
Alone, without consciousness,
Like a log.

—*DHAMMAPADA*, VERSE 41

No matter how much enemies harm enemies,
And haters harm haters,
The confused mind
Is the most harmful.

—*DHAMMAPADA*, VERSE 42

Zen Key

WHEN WE SEE the world dualistically—either/or—that's the very definition of confusion. When we observe all that arises with calm, nondiscriminating wisdom, we travel through the world undisturbed. The first practice of meditation is calming (*shamatha*). The second is looking deeply (*vipashyana*), seeing things as they are.

Reflection

Everyone has wars within. The practice is to stand your ground and not run away. Even living in an inner war zone, you can be like a lotus growing in the mud. Our inner conflicts don't have to hurt us. Others' hatred does not need to knock us down. These things can even nourish us and help us flourish. We don't need to surround ourselves with sycophants or even only with nice people. Our happiness does not depend on anything external. Peace comes from within. As long as we have room in our hearts for others to have their own views, they can't hurt us. A lotus in the mud is still a beautiful flower. We can live free of hatred, even among those who hate.

When someone says things you don't want to hear, when you feel misunderstood or unloved, *pause*. Be still and see what's happening. You're a free person, and you don't have to contest their opinions, but you can. You might say, for example, that they don't have to be afraid of immigrants and that immigrants have nothing to do with their suffering. When someone is unkind to you, they may be suffering themselves. When they blame or accuse you, pause, breathe, and give them love in return.

You can love them even when you feel ignored, misunderstood, or maligned. This is the Buddha's wisdom.

True strength is spacious. You don't need to defeat others to be free. You just need to stop receiving their projections as fact. When someone shouts, "You're wrong!" you don't have to shout back at them. You can stand like a tree and say, "I hear you," without abandoning yourself. This is not passivity; it's presence. When you stay present, you aren't adding more hatred to the world. And even if they never understand, something in the field lightens.

Mud is part of the earth. Conflict is part of awakening. We want to be surrounded by honest, kind people, but *being peace* does not depend on that. Real peace ripens in tension and shines in the midst of a storm. You can be the awareness that holds both sides of an argument. Your very presence can be a teaching. You are available, you are open, but you don't need to convince anyone of anything.

You don't need to fix others. Just sit there like the Buddha under the Bodhi tree. When Mara's arrows came, they became flowers. That is the secret: you don't need to win. You only have to pause and stay present. Stay with the truth; stay with your breath; stay open to love, even when your voice is shaking. The lotus is not afraid of the mud.

Part Three

The Wisdom of Flowers

Like bees alighting upon flowers,
Without disturbing their color or scent,
This is the way the Wise Ones
Move through the world.

—*DHAMMAPADA*, VERSE 49

17
Look Again

Like bees alighting upon flowers,
Without disturbing their color or scent,
Buzzing lightly above the petals, they drink only from the pistil.
This is the way the Wise Ones
Move through the world.

—*DHAMMAPADA*, VERSE 49

Don't look at others' faults,
What they have done or not done.
Look at yourself,
Is there anything you've left undone?

—*DHAMMAPADA*, VERSE 50

Zen Key

JUST AS BEES know how to respect flowers, we need to know how to respect our own minds. Every emotion needs to be felt in a gentle way. If we respect our inner world, we will respect the outer world. We don't look for others' faults but see their whole being through the eyes of compassion. Our own shortcomings, when we become aware of them, can encourage us to practice. Say hello to your whole self and give thanks for every step.

Reflection

When a thought or an emotion arises that causes so much pain that it's hard to bear, look again. When the world's politics keep you awake at night, see if you can find something else to focus on. There's no need to be in denial, but ingest your "medicine" in small doses. When pain is present, Eastern medicine says it's because your chi (energy) isn't flowing. You're stuck.

If you talk to your pain, you might discover that fear is at the root of it. You may be experiencing stress or even physical pain because you're afraid of something. Realizing that may be enough; the situation is in hand and the river of health can flow again. You are more than your fear. You are a buddha, connected to the cosmos. When you stop holding, when you stop resisting, fear no longer controls you.

The body may speak before the mind understands. A tightened chest, a clenched jaw—these are not problems to fix but messages to listen to. Breathe into the tension without judgment. Let the body speak, and let consciousness receive. Pain can become a bridge. When you stop running, you see that your hurt is the suffering of all beings. From that insight, compassion is born.

When life overwhelms you, return to something concrete: a leaf, the sound of the valley stream, a breath. The Dharma isn't an idea; it's aliveness, the relationship between your heart and the world. You are not here to improve. You're here to wake up. Touch one thing deeply, and freedom is at hand. Healing may be painful; a healing crisis might ensue. But if you stay with it, seeing that this itself is the path, something may open. This is the first noble truth: the truth not of comfort but of what is really happening, even when it's difficult. When you second-guess yourself and feel that all is hopeless, look again.

18
Experiencing Emptiness

Like a beautiful flower
With brilliant colors but no fragrance,
Well-spoken words without action
Are meaningless.

—*DHAMMAPADA*, VERSE 51

Like a beautiful flower
That's both colorful *and* fragrant,
Well-spoken words, when acted upon,
Can change lives.

—*DHAMMAPADA*, VERSE 52

Zen Key

THE FIRST ENNOBLING truth in Buddhism is that suffering exists. If we read the words without touching our own suffering deeply, we might think Buddhism is pessimistic. But the moment we actually touch our suffering, we also touch nonsuffering. Suffering is empty, and so is happiness. Talking about the four noble truths is not enough. The Dharma becomes real when we embody it in our lives.

Reflection

Thanks to *anatman*, "not-self," a connection between us is possible. Anatman is like good herbal medicine. When we take it, we're "cured." We no longer see ourselves as just an individual but instead as part of a network like mycelia. When someone else is happy, we feel joyful, too. When there is connection, life flows and we feel sympathetic joy for others' successes.

When they are suffering, we feel sad. It means there is connection, and with connection comes flow. When suffering flows, it's no longer only "my" suffering, and that alone provides ease. We experience something we didn't notice before. It was there, but we didn't see it. This is *shunyata*, emptiness. Thanks to emptiness, everything flows.

When we realize anatman, we still see characteristics like eye color, hair texture, and height, but we're not trapped by a confining image. We know then that we don't have to *look for* happiness, that we already have all that we're looking for. When we look at a flower, we see its beauty. When I look at you, I see your peace. When we touch this, we're no longer afraid of dark emotions.

And when we're no longer ashamed of parts of ourselves, the war within us stops. Emptiness means nonattachment to the positive or the negative. We see things as they are. We feel complete. Nothing needs to be larger or smaller. There is space for love and for happiness, because we're not holding on to anything too tightly. It's all part of a flowing completeness, like a flower with both color and scent.

Wholeness means we're not at war with others or with ourselves. When we let go of needing to be better, more spiritual, or more healed, we begin to see that everything we've been running from is a part of the path of the Dharma—the *Dhammapada*.

All flowers are okay as they are. The fragrance-free flower is beautiful, and the fragrant flower is beautiful. What is important is that our words, appearance, and actions are in alignment. Then we don't need to prove ourselves; we only need to embrace our body, feelings, and thoughts as they are, creating space for things to be themselves.

19
Holiness

From a gathering of petals,
Many lei can be strung.
With the deeds of your life,
Much good can be realized.
—*DHAMMAPADA*, VERSE 53

The fragrance of flowers
Doesn't fly upwind.
But the righteous act of an honorable person
Flows in all directions.
—*DHAMMAPADA*, VERSE 54

Zen Key

A FAMOUS Zen tale discusses good deeds vis-à-vis pride. Emperor Wu asked Bodhidharma, "What is the highest meaning of the holy truths?" and Bodhidharma replied, "Empty, without holiness." His answer was not a denial of holiness; it was in response to the emperor wanting to be praised for doing good works, building temples, and supporting Buddhism. Emperor Wu then asked, "Who is facing me?" and Bodhidharma replied, "I don't know."[12]

Flowers open slowly at first, and then suddenly they're in full bloom. Small deeds build a world worth living in. Change can feel like suffering, but ultimately, the fruit of a life well-lived is delicious and affects the whole world.

Reflection

I became a monk at the age of twenty-five and left the monastery at forty-one. After I left, I felt a lot of confusion. It took me a year to regain stability. There are forks in the road, and some paths end.

Bodhidharma meant, "You cannot grasp anything with concepts alone. Our essence is free from concepts." He felt Emperor Wu, despite his good deeds, was acting larger than life and not flowing with man's place in the scheme of things. Wu's concept of "good deeds," Bodhidharma observed, was keeping him from staying true to his big heart. I entered monastic life to realize Bodhidharma's understanding—the path to help us touch our true holiness. Holiness is what remains after we stop pretending. It's both simple and terrifying: It strips us of roles, titles, robes, gold stars, and even ideas of awakening.

After I left the monastery, I felt stripped of my identity. The rhythm of the daily life I had trusted was gone. The silence, once sacred, became heavy. But slowly, I began to see that the path had not ended; it was still visible, just harder to find. But like an underground river, it was still flowing.

The monastery had been my home, but I had mistaken the raft for the shore. Leaving didn't mean I was nowhere. It meant I was ready to live what I had learned, without relying as much on outer forms. The teachings were no longer gifted to me by the space, the sounds, and the community. Now they were in my breath, in how I met my confusion, in how I held my own hand when I didn't know what else to do. This is one way to look at not-self. In the *Dhammapada* verses, we're told the advantages of a life well-lived. But we're not warned of the pitfalls of confusing what we do with who we are.

Sooner or later, we have to leave everything behind: our roles, certainties, and communities. And what remains is the question, *When everything else is gone, who am I? What's left?* The answer comes by staying with yourself through all the transitions, trusting that the sacred doesn't disappear, it just changes form.

My true self and your true self are the same, and they bow to each other in silence. Sometimes, the bow is to continue the journey with no conclusion, no name, and no destination. Just step-by-step, breath-by-breath we return—not to what was but to what has always been.

20
Freedom from Truth

When a sage shows you where you're stuck,
It's like gifting you a buried treasure.
Stay close to these Wise Ones.
For your own well-being.
—*DHAMMAPADA*, VERSE 76

Zen Key

THE BUDDHA TAUGHT that one who sticks to dogmatic views, considering them the highest truth and thinking, "These are most excellent," while disparaging other views, is not a free person.[13] The Dharma doesn't give us the truth; it helps free us from it. If we apply this to daily life, we will loosen our grip on "truths" we hold dear, and in the process we may discover buried treasures. We need spiritual friends (*kalyanamitra*) to show us our "blind spots." We do well to stay close to such people, grateful for their honesty and their wisdom. Real friends don't just offer compliments; they also point out where we're stuck.

Reflection

When I was eight years old, North and South Vietnam were reunited, and four years later, in 1979, my family fled the country on a small boat. We were adrift on the huge ocean with little food or drink, and suddenly, we saw another boat. We thought it wouldn't be long before we could stand up and eat and laugh again. But the other vessel was a pirate ship, and they came to rob us of the funds we'd brought to build a new life. And they raped young women, sometimes in front of their families. The pirates left, and we sailed on, only to encounter another boat—more anticipation, and then more robberies and rapes.

Before we left South Vietnam, many people said, "How expensive is the price of freedom." I repeated those words without understanding them. My wife, who grew up in northern Vietnam after the war, heard different stories. One day, she asked me why the Americans had been in Vietnam. I said they were there to protect freedom. She replied, "The Americans bombed our country. We in the north had to endure their bombing day after day. More than a million civilians died, and you say it was to protect our freedom. How could that be? How can someone kill children and innocent civilians in the name of freedom?" To this day, "the price of freedom" is a "truth" that many overseas Vietnamese cling to. They suffered so much that they cannot let go of their *truth*.

Linji asked his teacher, "What is enlightenment? What is truth?" and his teacher hit him with a stick and told him to leave and take his questions with him. In the ninth century that was possible, but if such a thing happened today, I think Linji's teacher would be answering to the police. But it was a different time, and Linji asked his teacher the same question again, and a third time, and received the same response. After the third blow, he left the monastery, but before leaving he asked his teacher where he could go to study. His teacher suggested, "Go to Master Dayu. He is a good teacher."

Linji went to Master Dayu and told him what had happened. Master Dayu responded, "You have a great and compassionate teacher!" At that moment, Linji experienced enlightenment.

We may be suffering because we are caught by a particular truth, a bug in our bonnet. It may be partly true or wholly untrue, but other perspectives are also valid. In this sense, knowledge itself can be an obstacle. Thich Nhat Hanh said that in situations like that, even if truth were to come knocking at our door, we wouldn't let it in. We need to loosen our grip on what we know so we can broaden our perspective and find wisdom. The best teachers don't give their students knowledge. They take "knowing" away, freeing their students to see things as they are. This is exactly what Bodhidharma gifted Emperor Wu.

The more traumatized we are, the more tightly we hold on to our version of the truth. And that's understandable. Truth becomes a kind of protection, armor forged from real wounds. But at some point, it becomes too heavy. We carry it not because it helps us walk forward but because we're afraid to let it go.

That's why Master Dayu didn't offer Linji an answer, he offered space. Sometimes, what we need most is not confirmation, but interruption, something that stops the story long enough for other possibilities to emerge. In Zen, we speak of "not knowing" not as ignorance but as intimacy. When we let go of defending our views, we begin to see more clearly—not only the suffering of our side but the suffering of the other, and not only what was taken from us but what we're still holding on to.

Freedom is not a flag. It's not a slogan. It's the ability to listen without fear, to be touched by someone's pain, even when it challenges our beliefs. That is true courage. I still carry the memories of that ocean and what was done to us. And I still carry my wife's question. Both are real. Both belong. Neither needs to be erased.

To be free is not to forget but to stop being trapped by our version of the past. When we loosen our grip on truth, we begin to touch understanding. This is where healing begins.

21
The Path of Practice

Those who support wholesome behavior
And keep us from crossing lines
Are admired by the wise
While despised by bad actors.
—*DHAMMAPADA*, VERSE 77

Zen Key

HAVING A TEACHER is an important part of the path of practice. We need teachers who can advise and support us, who believe in our capacity to become buddhas. A good teacher is a link to all teachers who have ever lived. Thich Nhat Hanh once told me, "One day, my body won't be here anymore. Make sure your body becomes my body, and your mind becomes my mind."

Reflection

After his enlightenment, the Buddha encountered the five men he had been practicing asceticism with, and they greeted him as a friend. The Buddha said, "I come now as a teacher." It may seem arrogant, but he had to say so. He'd had a profound insight he wanted to share with them. His friends listened to the Buddha's first "sermon" at the Deer Park in Sarnath, near Varanasi. The moment a friend becomes a teacher is not about status. It's about insight and the willingness to share your newly deepened understanding. Thich Nhat Hanh said, "A good teacher is someone who can help you . . . touch the true teacher within, because you already have the insight within you."[14]

When I teach, I don't feel above anyone. I feel responsible for passing on what I've seen and experienced. Teaching is not about transmitting ideas; it's about walking alongside others with openness and presence. Sometimes that means sitting silently with them. Sometimes it means saying what they don't want to hear. A good teacher doesn't perform or even impart wisdom. They embody care.

I didn't plan to become a teacher. I only knew I needed to walk the path of the Dharma, and I still do. When someone calls me thây, the Vietnamese word for teacher, I receive it as a reminder to be real, honest, and clear. A teacher who forgets they are also a student has lost their way.

Thây Nhat Hanh taught us that the teacher is inside. A real teacher helps you return not to them but to yourself. If, after meeting a teacher, someone is more at peace with themselves, the teacher has done something meaningful. They've helped them see what they already had. You may not think of yourself as a teacher, but when you live from insight and tenderness, others will learn from you. They may not call you "teacher," but they will recognize something and benefit from it.

Teachers don't need big crowds. The Buddha's first teaching had an audience of five, and it was not complicated. He said, "There is suffering and a path that leads out of it." That is the true teaching, a path we can all walk.

22
Sangha Building

Don't cozy up to the ill-intentioned
Or be friends with dishonest ones.
Stay close to spiritual friends
And those who act with nobility.

—*DHAMMAPADA*, VERSE 78

Zen Key

WHEN WE FEEL unsure of ourselves, a sangha can help guide us through. We can rely on the power of the connection and support that comes from practicing with others. The word *sangha* traditionally referred to the community of monastics training under the guidance of the Buddha or one of his disciples. Today it refers to any community of copractitioners who encourage each other along the path. Some sanghas meditate together on a regular basis; some have other practices as well.

At the end of a Day of Mindfulness near San Francisco, Thich Nhat Hanh told the thousands of people gathered,

"If a sangha is available in your area, please keep in touch and take refuge there. . . . The art of sangha building is crucial to our practice."[15] We need to stay connected with others who can help us deepen our understanding and compassion.

Reflection

After the Buddha's enlightenment, a community of disciples formed around him. Many of them came together for the monsoon season. Practicing together, they listened to the Buddha share his insights, and they supported each other. Over time, some of these communities continued year-round. The Buddha recognized that practicing in community gives us stability, support, and love. A sangha is not a place where everyone believes in one dogmatic truth. We come together to be present for each other, and when someone is suffering, we give our attention to their suffering and, when requested, share our insight. Over time, practicing with a sangha can help us develop trust in ourselves and others.

In community, your suffering is not just yours. It is held by the collective not to be fixed but to be seen. And the joy that arises is shared, too. In a true community, you don't have to speak much. Just being there is enough. When you sit together in silence, breathing mindfully, you are already sharing something real. A sangha is made of human beings, and so, of course, there will be misunderstandings, discomfort, and differences. But that is the "stuff" of the practice, and we learn to listen, to stay, and to see the Buddha in the person who irritates us. We let go of the idea that harmony means sameness.

You may be part of a formal sangha, or you may be practicing with one friend or even just by yourself with the earth beneath you. A sangha is not an escape from life but a way to live more deeply. What matters is intention. Thich Nhat Hanh introduced the idea that the next Buddha—Maitreya, the Buddha of friendship—may take the form of a sangha. A few people sitting together, embodying the Dharma, are enough to keep the flame alive.

23
Delighting in the Dharma

Practicing the Dharma brings peace
And a clear mind.
The wise enjoy the stability of stillness
Practicing the Buddha's Way

—*DHAMMAPADA*, VERSE 79

Zen Key

THE BUDDHA TAUGHT the three marks of existence. One is anatman, or not-self. This is not the denial of a self but a recognition of interbeing. This Dharma seal goes hand in hand with the Buddha's teachings on impermanence (*anitya*) and suffering (*dukkha*), the other two marks of existence. When we suffer and know that we are suffering, we already experience joy. Seeing impermanence, we can let go of our attachments, and joy comes by itself.

Reflection

When the Buddha meditated on the *body,* he saw that it is already decomposing. We know now that in just seven years, our bodies completely renew themselves. But even then, it was clear to him that a decomposing body could not be an "I." We can enjoy ourselves and our children without thinking we "own" them, that they're "ours." The same is true of our relationship to our self. We don't own even our own self. Thanks to anatman, we have the freedom to respect ourselves without the onus of ownership.

Buddha also saw that every *feeling* is empty of an "I," so there is no need to hold on to pleasant feelings or avoid unpleasant ones. When you understand that there's no "I" in your feelings, you can *be with* your feelings without being "in control."

And the Buddha saw that there is no "I" in *mind*. When you see thoughts as reified truths, you are creating a self. Insight frees us from believing that our thoughts are the truth. The more attached we are to our knowledge, the more difficult it is to learn something new. When we know that there is no independent, permanent "I," it creates space. No "I," just respect, and all conflicts are put to rest.

Letting go of the "I" doesn't make us disappear; it

makes us free. When you don't have to protect a fixed self, you can relax, your breath can deepen, and your heart can become more available. Suddenly, there's space for joy, sorrow, and not-knowing. The idea of ownership—"this is my body," "my child," "my anger," or even "my truth"—can be a burden. When we say "my," we grasp. When we say "this simply is," we allow. This shift in perspective is everything.

I see people suffer when they're convinced they need to defend their opinions. But when they look more deeply, they can't find anything solid. With no "I" to protect and nothing to defend, freedom arises. We may think, "This shouldn't be happening to me," but if it's life just happening, suffering will loosen its grip. Thanks to anatman, we can be more real, connected, and humble. We don't need to win; we only need to breathe, walk, and be present with things as they are. When there's no "I" to defend, listening deepens and compassion arises naturally. Peace becomes possible not as a belief but as a lived experience.

24
The Nature of Things

A levee maker regulates the flow of water.
An arrowsmith crafts arrows,
A carpenter works wood,
While the wise hone themselves.

—*DHAMMAPADA*, VERSE 80

Like a boulder
The wind can't budge,
The wise are unmoved
By praise or blame.

—*DHAMMAPADA*, VERSE 81

Zen Key

THERE IS a Buddhist teaching called the eight worldly winds, which are gain and loss, success and failure, praise and blame, and pleasure and pain. The wise ones are not afraid of these dyads and meet them with equanimity. These women and men know who they are and don't need to prove themselves. Dogen wrote, "To study the buddha way is to study the self. To study the self is to forget the self. To forget the self is to be actualized by myriad things."[16] The teaching of not-self helps us understand our relationship with the world. Looking deeply into our own nature and the nature of the universe, we observe the myriad things enlightening us all the time. So, to understand the "great matter," we focus on ourselves—our own body and mind.

Reflection

If you work out at a gym, after a while what used to be heavy is no longer heavy. Your weight-lifting capacity increases. In the same way, an untrained mind may lack self-control, rushing toward what you like and pushing away what you don't, tossed about by the eight worldly winds. But with practice, even a short retreat, you can learn to *be peace* and touch the profound silence within you. When you learn to pause and stop discriminating between gain and loss, success and failure, praise and blame, and pleasure and pain, you are already on the path of transformation.

The Sanskrit term *smriti* (*sati* in Pali) means "mindfulness" or "to remember." Just as an embankment engineer tends the flow of water and a woodworker makes beautiful objects out of wood, we take care of ourselves. With mindfulness, we still feel gain and loss, praise and blame, but they don't shake us the same way. We have a place to stand. Mindfulness is not about achieving a special state. It's about becoming simple again— breathing, sitting, and washing our hands with attention.

I grew up in a time of war. No one can win a war. An alternative is mindfulness. With mindful awareness, we can learn to modulate impulses and stop the wars, beginning with the wars within us. The peace we long for is already here, if we take the time to stop and appreciate life. I've seen people who have never meditated before attend a retreat, and by the second day, they look different. Their eyes are softer, their breathing slower not because their problems disappeared but because they're no longer fighting with themselves. That is the power of remembering.

Even one mindful breath can open a door. You remember your body. You remember that you don't need to get anywhere. You still feel sad or overwhelmed, but now it has space. Mindfulness doesn't get rid of pain; it helps us hold the pain without identifying with it. When we're mindful, our friends and family feel it. The practice is not self-centered; it's deeply relational. When we remember ourselves, we remember each other. We don't need to wait for the perfect conditions. In this present moment, we can touch our next inhalation and exhalation. That's enough. You're already in training. This is the beginning of freedom.

25
The Pathway to Peace

Like a deep lake
Is clear and placid,
Hearing the Dharma
Brings lucidity and peace.
—*DHAMMAPADA*, VERSE 82

Zen Key

SOMETIMES WE LOOK for happiness by avoiding suffering or trying to defeat it. This never works. Peace is beyond "this versus that." It's attainable only when we release our desire for happiness and let go of our wish to overcome suffering. When our minds are clear and not grasping at straws, we know when suffering is present, and we know when happiness is present. We don't discriminate; we build capacity.

•

Reflection

Many people work day and night to attain position, power, or financial security. And before they know it, life is coming to a close and much has been left unattended. Our bodies change or plans change or hopes change. Like a flower, we can't live forever. Both we and flowers decompose. Looking for a particular idea of happiness can lead us astray, as we overlook resonance and opportunities to push ahead toward our goal. Self-compassion while being present with things as they are provides a more reliable pathway to peace.

Presence can be enough. When we stop reaching for something "better," we begin to see what's already here. We think peace is something we'll reach once everything settles down. But life never settles for long. The moon waxes and wanes. The flower opens and fades. What matters is not how long something lasts but whether we're present while it's here. We don't need to hold on to anything. We only need to be present for it. Self-compassion means not waiting to become someone else before being kind to yourself. It means seeing that who you are right now is worthy of care. Not because you've done something right but because you're alive. Sometimes practice is simply remembering that you're sitting, breathing, and feeling your feet on the floor. You don't have to fix your life or figure everything out. You only need to stop and see. Allow yourself to be touched by this moment not because it will last forever but because it's already enough.

Part Four

Liberation

Those who practice the Way,
According to the well-taught Dharma,
Overcome all obstacles
And reach the other shore.

—*DHAMMAPADA*, VERSE 86

26
The Joy of Equanimity

Those who live mindfully are equanimous.
They don't hold on to preferences,
Nor pleasure or pain,
Joy or sadness.
—*DHAMMAPADA*, VERSE 83

Zen Key

EVERYTHING YOU NEED is already available. You just need to open your senses and see and feel. You don't need to fill the space with words or hold on to anything. When *stillness* permeates your body and mind, even though suffering is there, you don't need to suffer. And when happiness is there, you don't need to ascend or be transported. Simply pause and stay with yourself, savoring each moment with your whole heart. This is the joy of equanimity.

Reflection

Distraction causes a lot of our suffering. We ignore what's here now as though it's not enough, and we imagine something else we think would be better. Even if our hearts are open and we're trying to contribute to others' well-being, we blot out what is in front of us, ignoring things as they are.

The wise ones are diligent and brave, practicing true presence. Open the door to your experience, whatever it is, and feel the joy that arises. This is beyond happiness or suffering. As noted earlier, Chinese ancestor Sengcan said, "The Great Way is not difficult / for those who have no preferences. / When love and hate are both absent, / everything becomes clear and undisguised." That happiness is always available, but we miss it when we're trying to avoid discomfort. Staying present with things as they are is a kind of training; it's training our mind to be equanimous. Doing so, we become resilient and resourceful.

"Being with" does not mean liking or agreeing with everything. It means accepting what is, including fear, disappointment, and restlessness. Staying present with our suffering, we stop looking for a perpetrator to blame, and when we do so, something inside us shifts. We can breathe again and see that what we were avoiding is approachable. Difficulties don't need to be pushed aside. They want to be companioned. We can train ourselves not to run away.

Equanimity is not numbness. It's playful and passionate, yet relaxed and truly present. It becomes possible when we let go of the idea that things should be different, and in that letting go, a peace that's deeper than trying arrives. We practice not to attain something outside ourselves or to go somewhere else but to return—to our breathing, to ourselves, and to each other. This is the beginning of a new day.

27
The Other Shore

Few among us
Reach the other shore.
The rest
Scurry to and fro on this side.

—*DHAMMAPADA*, VERSE 85

Those who practice the Way,
According to the well-taught Dharma,
Overcome all obstacles
And reach the other shore.

—*DHAMMAPADA*, VERSE 86

Zen Key

The Heart of the Prajñaparamita is a beautiful sutra chanted daily at Zen centers and monasteries throughout the world. *Prajña* means "insight" and *paramita* means "reaching the other shore" or, literally, "transcendence" or "perfection." This Mahayana scripture describes the wisdom that can set us free and take us to "the other shore," a state beyond greed, hatred, and ignorance, a world at peace filled with joy.

Reflection

The moment we discover suffering as an ennobling truth, we have insight, and what have been obstacles lose their power over us. On the other shore, suffering and happiness inter-are. You cannot have either without experiencing both.

I've met seekers who know a lot about the Dharma but little about their own suffering. They think the other shore is a place where only happiness exists. It takes courage to change this goal, see the ways you are suffering, and realize that nonduality is the point. The moment you *see* your suffering is the moment of awakening, the moment you cross the river and arrive at the other shore.

Awakening doesn't need to take years. Sometimes a single honest moment when you stop running, performing, or trying to prove something is enough. Simply sit with what is hurting. The Buddha didn't tell us to get rid of suffering. He said we should understand it. And when you do, it begins to transform. It doesn't disappear, but it loosens its grip. If you can sit with one wound without judgment, you're on the path of compassion, approaching the other shore. You don't have to run away anymore. You can hold adversity without falling to pieces.

Sometimes insight arrives quietly, in the pause between thoughts or between breaths. It may arrive in a single teardrop. Suddenly you can feel and see. Equanimity is not dissociated coolness but the warmth and courage of awakening to what is present. When the Buddha saw suffering, he didn't turn away. His smile is trustworthy. If we can offer others understanding, that is powerful medicine.

28
There's Nothing That Is Always Good

Arriving at our destination,
No more sorrow, liberation beyond liberation.
All burdens released,
Freed from the embers of suffering.

—*DHAMMAPADA*, VERSE 90

Zen Key

WE WANT to be free of sorrow, illusions, and the ties that weigh us down. Letting go of our "truths" is a good starting place. Open yourself to new perspectives, new ways of seeing, as you arrive "home," which is the source and the essence of all.

Reflection

We want goodness, purity, health, and happiness, but these desires are all one-sided. If we look closely at wellness, traces of disease are always present, too. If we look at living, hints of death are already here. If we look at the good, we see what is bad as well. Some religions promise eternal life, but nothing lasts forever. Nothing is always good. There is no place we can be only healthy and only happy.

Impermanence can seem scary, but there's no need to be afraid of it. Change is life's flow itself, not our enemy. Even the things we cherish—our health, our loved ones, our insights—are not meant to stay forever. They touch us, teach us, and move along. You might be reading this book to become happier or a better person, but you are never just happy or good. Suzuki Roshi said, "Each of you is perfect the way you are, and you can use a little improvement."[17] The practice is not to be healthy and happy all the time but to be ourselves. The moment we accept body and mind as they are, we are free. When we know this deeply, we stop clinging. We don't need things to last forever. We just need to be present while they're happening.

When you can see the suffering inside of happiness and the happiness inside of suffering, you'll be able to relax. You stop hoping for one without the other. You stop expecting life to be clean and controlled. Instead, you become spacious, willing to feel what's true.

Some people worry that if they accept impermanence, they will sink into despair. But the opposite is true. When you no longer expect permanence, you begin to love honestly. You can *appreciate* without grasping, hold without trying to possess. In *The Heart of the Buddha's Teaching*, Thich Nhat Hanh wrote,

> We can practice conscious breathing to help us be in touch with things and to look deeply at their impermanent nature. This practice will keep us from complaining that everything is impermanent and therefore not worth living for. Impermanence is what makes transformation possible. We should learn to say, "Long live impermanence." Thanks to impermanence, we can change suffering into joy.[18]

This is a different kind of happiness—one that is not based on getting what you want but on being open to what is. You don't have to wait until you are wise to practice this. You can begin now. Notice how thoughts, moods, and sounds come and go. Even your idea of who you are will change if you allow it to. There is peace in seeing clearly, and clarity is not hard to attain. It just takes a little space, a little stillness to see that you are already perfect in your changing. And that is enough.

29
Where the Rubber Meets the Road

Practicing mindfulness,
We needn't look for any other home.
Like migratory swans flocking from a muddy pool,
We leave each shelter behind.

—*DHAMMAPADA*, VERSE 91

Zen Key

WE DON'T NEED to build a palace to be happy. We can focus on freedom, like a wild swan, present for each experience without grasping or attachment and following the patterns of the wind.

Reflection

Without knowing illness, we cannot know the value of health. We don't have to look for disease, but when we're sick, we have an increased appreciation for well-being. The same is true of death. If we don't know death, we cannot fully appreciate life.

After living as a monk in Plum Village, I left the community and felt like a failure. I saw the monks and nuns I'd left behind as pure and good and myself as less than. I knew I wanted to marry and have children, although I didn't have a girlfriend at the time. My Dharma brothers criticized me: "You've been a monk for sixteen years, and now you want a wife and children. You should be free of worldly things." I felt alone.

One night a year later, I woke up feeling deeply conflicted inside, and then suddenly I could see clearly that I was *empty*—empty of success and empty of failure. For sixteen years, I believed I could cultivate the positive and overcome the negative through monastic living. I'd been designing a palace where I would always be free from suffering, but that night I saw that such a palace does not exist. A huge burden was lifted from my shoulders.

When you discover that you are empty of purity, you realize you've reached a dead end. There is no path to purity, and you've been living in constant fear of impurity. Then one day you get stuck in the mud with no way out. When that happens, don't try to run away. Be still and stay where you are. *This* is "home," and there is no escape. Stay calm (or shake, if you will, but stay present) until you discover the beauty in the dread and the gift of not-knowing. In that moment, you can see a path that lifts the iron veil between right and wrong, good and evil, you and life. That night, I knew I no longer had to improve myself or prove anything to anyone, including myself. I gasped; I could breathe again—not because I'd arrived but because I stopped *trying* to arrive. Till then, becoming worthy had been my project. But worthiness built on a foundation of fear is not freedom. It's another prison.

The Buddha didn't say we have to become good. He taught us to see clearly. And that night when I saw clearly, I realized that purity and impurity are ideas I had, like old robes that no longer fit. I could shed them and trust myself again—not who I thought I should be but who I am, imperfect and uncertain.

We don't need to build palaces. We can sit in the ruins and feel the breeze across our cheek. Stay where you are in the middle of your so-called failure and realize it's not failure, it's a gate. The dead end is not a cul-de-sac. It's the very place where the rubber meets the road. Once you stop "efforting," something opens. You can feel the ground and see the sky again. You're no longer trying to be anyone else. The Buddha's path doesn't lead away from your life; it brings you back into it.

30
Victory

Even better than vanquishing a thousand enemies
On a thousand battlefields,
True victory
Is when we "conquer" ourselves.

—*DHAMMAPADA*, VERSE 103

Self-conquest is greater
Than defeating others.
Those who "win" themselves
Live in peace.

—*DHAMMAPADA*, VERSE 104

Zen Key

I WAS A CHILD during the Vietnam War. Now I teach Buddhism in the West, and the teaching I most want to share is how to stop the wars inside of you. To me, spiritual practice is, first and foremost, the emptying of one's self. The Buddha called this "non-self." Thich

Nhat Hanh introduced the term *interbeing*. In Zen, we say "not two and not one." Only when I am empty of Cuong, empty of the identity of being a teacher, can I be myself. A leaf is not just a leaf. It is also the tree and also the earth.

Reflection

In Vietnam, we used well water for drinking, bathing, and washing clothes. There is a famous story of a man who went to his neighborhood well to get water for cooking. He saw a pair of pants draped over the edge and began shouting loudly, perhaps suspecting his wife was having an affair. Then he realized they were his own pants; he'd left them there that morning after washing.

All wars begin inside us. When we look deeply within, we discover the presence of our ancestors. We are not separate from the world and history. We were never isolated individuals. The wisdom of "no birth, no death" is a gateway to liberation, a path to the roots of our existence and the unbreakable connections among living beings. When we let go of the idea of ourselves as isolated individuals, we free ourselves from the chains of illusion and experience wisdom and compassion, focusing on the big picture in which we and others live in harmony. This "victory" is a source of peace and true happiness. We're no longer at war with ourselves. Like the man at the well, when we lose mindfulness, we blame the world, but when we stop and look deeply, we see that the person we're angry with is us. No one wins when we shout at our own pants.

We carry the stories of our ancestors, and we also carry their strengths, dreams, and resilience. We are not alone, and when we understand this, compassion arises naturally. The people we resented become a part of us. The anger that consumed us begins to soften. We no longer need to win. We just need to see clearly, and in that seeing, the struggle ends.

Every moment we return to presence, we are victorious, not over others, but over delusion. Our pants are still there, ready for us to take them home. And the well water is cool and clear.

31
Homecoming

How wonderful it is to live
Free from illness among so many who are ill.
Surrounded by illness,
We can learn to stay well.
—*DHAMMAPADA*, VERSE 198

How great to live
Free from greed among so many
who are greedy.
Surrounded by greed,
We live modestly, generous of spirit.
—*DHAMMAPADA*, VERSE 199

Zen Key

YOUR CONSTITUTION is healthy; your mind has the capacity to flow. Health can be found, even in illness. In a world where so many are unwell and those who have so much always want more, we can drop into a deeply still place. Zen master Tran Nhan Tong taught, "Our bodies are in the city; our minds are in the forest."

Reflection

When I was five years old, I got lost. I was just two hundred yards from my house, but I didn't know how to get home. I cried and was very scared. A man asked me why I was crying, and I said I wanted to be at home with my father. He asked my father's name, and when I told him, he said, "Oh, I know where you live. I'll take you there." I sat on his Vespa scooter, and within a minute I was home.

"Home" is an apt image for the deep stillness that's available even in the midst of greed, hatred, and delusion. To find our way home, we may need a teacher, directions, and the support of friends. These are the Three Jewels: Buddha, Dharma, and Sangha. When we feel burdened by what is in our heart, taking refuge in these jewels can be a kind of life support.

You can always find peace "at home." But when you don't remember the way back, sit on my Vespa, and I'll get you there in a minute. It's okay if you don't remember the way; someone can help you. When we practice meditation, our nervous system calms and our life energy flows. We become healthier and, in a sense, we grow younger. "Doing nothing" eases the conflicts in your heart.

The Buddha didn't build us a house. He described the path home. It can take the form of a friend's hand, a cushion, or your next aware breath. We can walk home slowly or take a scooter, which may appear in the form of a poem, a cup of tea, or leaves rustling in the wind. Any of these vehicles can help us get home. And if you still feel lost, ask for help. Someone, somewhere, knows the way.

At home, you don't have to prove yourself. You're always welcome. That is the power of refuge. You don't need to be fearless; you only need to be willing. Intention opens the gate, and when you enter, you'll realize you were never really away.

32
Choose Love

How nice to live,
Free of possessions,
Dwelling in joy
Like the gods in the heavens.
—*DHAMMAPADA*, VERSE 200

Zen Key

WE CAN let go of attachments—and especially of "things as they aren't"—and return to joy and peace. When our mind is controlled by desire, even if we think we're moving toward happiness, it inevitably leads to suffering. The practice is to choose love, to see the perfection in everything.

Reflection

If your mind is untrained, you run after your latest desires and acquire physical objects, people, or ideals, what Chögyam Trungpa called "spiritual materialism." You are already wealthy, and the more you give away, the richer you become. In the *Lotus Sutra*, a bodhisattva appears and bows to everyone. Wherever she looks, she sees a buddha. You can do that, too. Whoever you meet in life, you can choose to see their beauty, a priceless gift for you both. This is *dana paramita*, a gift that brings you both to the other shore. When you recognize the Buddha in others, they recognize the Buddha in themselves.

It is possible to live in a world where everyone is perfect just as they are. We don't only wish it; we actually *see* it. Nothing needs to be changed; nothing needs to be bigger or smaller. Dare to live that way for even a day, seeing the perfection that is already here, recognizing how beautiful the world and others already are.

Generosity doesn't begin with what we have. It begins with what we see. When we recognize the Buddha in another person, we stop trying to fix them. We stop needing them to be different. Our gift doesn't have to be material. It can be a glance, a warm hello, or a spacious silence. These are offerings placed on the altar of life, and they say, "I see you. You are already whole."

Practice doing this for a day. Without trying to fix or change anything, just look. Look at someone's hands, their eyes, their way of being. There's no need to label or compare. Just see them as they are, beyond the roles they play or what you might want from them. Just this moment, this breath. And when you do, you'll feel a shift in them and in you, not something dramatic but the realization that they are enough.

You may not feel you have much to offer. You might feel tired or sad, but even your tiredness is an offering when held with honesty and care. The Buddha didn't say to become someone else. He told us to wake up to what's here. When we see the world as already beautiful, we stop trying to manipulate it. We stop conquering, exploiting, and extracting. And the world feels it and gives back her bounty out of love. She seeks no applause, just living in peace together, grateful and generous and brave of heart. This is real wealth. This is generosity.

33
Be Yourself and Your Non-Self at the Same Time

The Sage, victorious
A hero, a great person,
Purified, awakened,
Untainted, cleansed,
A true practitioner of the Way.

—*DHAMMAPADA*, VERSE 422

The Accomplished know their past,
See heaven and hell clearly,
Have stopped the cycle of birth and death,
Attained wisdom and eradicated the defilements.
They have completed all there is to do.
They are true practitioners of the Way.

—*DHAMMAPADA*, VERSE 423

Zen Key

THE FINAL CHAPTER of the *Dhammapada* is called "The Brahmin." In Buddhism, a *brahmin* is someone who is peaceful, friendly toward others, content with little, and free from greed, hatred, and delusion. These last two verses of the *Dhammapada* extol the accomplishments of those who have attained the Great Way.

Reflection

When my teacher, Thich Nhat Hanh, passed away, I cried a lot. I had come to him as a young man and was ordained by him as a Buddhist monk more than thirty years ago. Although he has gone beyond, he is still with me today. Even now, we practice together and are connected. There is no separation between us; we share timelessness and also spacelessness. If you look at me, you will see yourself, your beloved spouse, your children, Thich Nhat Hanh, all the great beings, and even Mara. We inter-are. Thich Nhat Hanh is not just in the past. He is here—in my breath, in your steps, and every time you remember to come back to yourself. We don't need to look for him in memories. When we are fully present, he is here.

When you walk gently, when you listen deeply, your

teacher, your ancestors, and your beloved are walking with you, listening to you. This is the truth of interbeing. If you greet yourself each morning with kindness, you will never be far from the path. Even when things fall apart, even when grief returns, your breath remains steady, and in that breath, the world returns.

Sometimes we feel lonely, but we are never really alone. We are held by the earth, the sky, by every person we have ever loved and lost. The moment we remember this, we begin again. Compassion is reborn not as a task but as a song.

Don't try to fix your life. Just return to it. Sit. Breathe. Smile—even a small smile. Thây is smiling with you. This is how the world renews: not with a revolution but with a breath. Not with perfection, but with presence. We are not here to impress anyone. We are here to love and be loved, to suffer and be healed, to walk the path with our own two feet and discover again and again that the path is made by walking. Dhammapada—the path of the Dharma, the way of understanding and love.

Breathe in and out and be yourself and your non-self at the same time. Doing this, you are complete. When you wake up in the morning, practice mindful breathing and greet yourself by name. Why? To remind yourself that you are important. Remember the moment you met your beloved. Try to feel that way about yourself.

Then when life is difficult for you or your beloved, you know how to return home to yourself. Nourish the energy of love and the energy of insight, and others will feel it. A new world is possible, and it starts with you.

Afterword
Returning to What Matters

THIS BOOK does not come from me. It comes from a man who walked barefoot through forests and sat quietly beneath trees many years ago. He was born into this world like all of us: fragile, curious, searching. And what he, the Buddha, discovered wasn't a religion. He discovered you.

The Buddha's greatest feat wasn't just enlightenment. He discovered that breath is sacred, that confusion is part of the path, and that tears are not signs of weakness but of freedom. Everything we carry—joy, fear, tenderness, and grief—is already enough. This is not an idea. It is a lived truth. I've spent more than thirty years walking with the Buddha, and I begin anew each morning.

When I look back at my life, I don't see a succession of achievements. I see small, silent moments when I've remembered who I am and who I am not. And I've felt the support of so many people. As a child, as a monk at Plum Village, and as a husband and a father, it still means a lot to me when someone holds my hand and reminds me to forgive myself for not being further along the path of understanding and love. And when I look into someone's eyes—a prisoner, a friend, a student—and see that they, too, are just trying to be free, I feel a part of a greater universe.

I wrote this book to share the teachings of the *Dhammapada*. These teachings do not offer perfection. They offer presence. This is not a rulebook. It's a mirror reflecting back your struggles, possibilities, and attainments. It reminds us that peace is not something we discover anew; it's something we return to.

It's okay to feel unsure. You do not need to wear special robes to walk this path. You don't need to retreat from life, from feelings, from your own inner turmoil. You only need to be sincere, to bow deeply to what is, to listen, to discern, and to begin anew again and again.

If I have succeeded, it's because I didn't teach you anything new. I helped you remember your breath, your dignity, and the ground beneath your feet. We are already home. We always were.

As you close this book, remember the vast teachings in the *Dhammapada*. Whether you reread a verse a day or just go sit by a tree, the Dharma is alive in you. Knowing that fills me with joy.

Notes

1. *The Dhammapada: The Path of Truth,* trans by Ven. Balangoda Ananda Maitreya and Rose Kramer, rev. ed. (Parallax Press, 2001), xvi.
2. H.H. the Dalai Lama and Howard C. Cutler, MD, *The Art of Happiness: A Handbook for Living* (Riverhead, 1998), 200.
3. Michael Kearney, *Luminous Resilience* (forthcoming).
4. Thich Nhat Hanh, *The Diamond That Cuts Through Illusion*, rev. ed. (Parallax Press, 2006), 67. Italics added.
5. John, 14.6.
6. "Anyone who has seen me has seen the Father," John 14:9. "When you look at yourself, you see me," a paraphrase based on the Christian ideal that through faith you become a reflection of Jesus's teachings and example.
7. Thich Nhat Hanh, *The Heart of the Buddha's Teaching* (Broadway Books, 1999), 124.
8. This story is from Nikos Kazantzakis, *Saint Francis* (Loyola University Press, 2005) and quoted in Thich Nhat Hanh, *Living Buddha, Living Christ*, 20th anniversary ed. (Riverhead Books, 2007), 43.
9. Nyanaponika Thera, *The Roots of Good and Evil* (Buddhist Publication Society, 2008), 22.
10. Gabor Maté, "Trauma Is Not What Happens to You, It's What Happens Inside You," video posted July 22, 2021, by Skoll, YouTube, www.youtube.com/watch?v=nmJOuTAko9g.

11. Richard B. Clarke, trans., *Hsin Hsin Ming*, in Mu Soeng, *Trust in Mind* (Wisdom Publications, 2004), 13.
12. Thomas and J. C. Cleary, trans., *The Blue Cliff Record* (Prajña Press, 1977), 1.
13. *Paramatthaka Sutta, Sutta Nipāta*, 4.5, Plum Village, accessed November 25, 2025, https://plumvillage.org/library/sutras/discourse-on-the-absolute-truth.
14. Thich Nhat Hanh, interview by bell hooks, "Building a Community of Love," *Lion's Roar*, January 20, 2025, www.lionsroar.com/bell-hooks-thich-nhat-hanh-building-community-love.
15. Thich Nhat Hanh, "The Next Buddha May Be a Sangha," *Inquiring Mind* 10, no. 12 (Spring 1994), https://inquiringmind.com/article/1002_41_thich-nhat_hanh/.
16. Dogen, "Actualizing the Fundamental Point," trans. Kazuaki Tanahashi and Robert Aitken Roshi, in Kazuaki Tanahashi, ed., *Enlightenment Unfolds: The Essential Teachings of Zen Master Dogen* (Shambhala Publications, 1999), 56.
17. Shunryu Suzuki, *Zen Mind, Beginner's Mind* (Shambhala Publications, 1970), 92.
18. Thich Nhat Hanh, *The Heart of the Buddha's Teaching* (Broadway Books, 1997), 133.

About the Author

Cuong Lu, Buddhist teacher, scholar, and writer, was born in Nha Trang, Vietnam, in 1968 and emigrated to the Netherlands with his family in 1980. He majored in East Asian studies at the University of Leiden, and in 1993 was ordained as a monk at Plum Village in France under the guidance of Thich Nhat Hanh. In 2000, he was recognized as a teacher in the Lieu Quan line of the Linji School of Zen Buddhism.

In 2009, Cuong left Plum Village after sixteen years and returned to lay life in the Netherlands. He served as a chaplain in Holland's penitentiary system for six years. In 2015, he received a master's degree in Buddhist spiritual care at Vrije (Free) University in Amsterdam. Cuong is the founder of the Mind Only school, in Gouda, the Netherlands, where he teaches Buddhist philosophy and psychology, specializing in Yogachara Buddhism combined with the Madhyamaka (Middle Way) School of

Nagarjuna. He is also the founder of the No Word Zen order of "invisible monastics," and the No Word Zen Practice Center in Magnac-Laval, France.

Cuong leads retreats and gives Dharma talks in Europe, the United States, and Asia and offers presentations to large organizations. He is the author of *The Buddha in Jail: Restoring Lives, Finding Hope and Freedom*; *Wait: A Love Letter to Those in Despair*; and *Happiness Is Overrated: Simple Lessons on Finding Meaning in Each Moment*. Visit https://nowordzen.com.